Copyright © 2019

All rights reserved. No part of this publication may be reproduced, distributed, or transmitted in any form or by any means, including photocopying, recording, or other electronic or mechanical methods, without the prior written permission of the publisher.

D1314189

COMPLIMENT MY BUTT, HUMAN

You
Can Look,
But no
touchie!

ENJOY
THE VIEW

I CAN'T SEE IT.
WHAT DOES IT LOOK LIKE?

WHY CAN'T YOU JUST BE GRATEFUL FOR THE VIEW ???

CENSORED
NO FREE SHOWS

NO
FLASH
catography
PLEASE

I'M IGNORING YOU NOW

MY BUTT likes you, HUMAN

HUMAN
WE REQIRE
YOUR
ASSISTANCE

GREETINGS
STUPID
HUMAN!

CAN'T HELP
THAT
IT'S
BEAUTIFUL

you're lucky
YOU GET
TO VIEW
it

I SHOW YOU
MY BUTT
BECAUSE
I CARE

I'M LOCKED and LOADED
CAREFUL

stand AT attention
PLEASE!

I LOVE CAT BUTTS AND I CANNOT LIE

I REQUIRE YOUR ATTENTION

TELL ME
IS MY BUTT
TOO BIG?
I CAN
TAKE IT...

HEY!
EYES
UP
HERE

ISN'T IT marvelous?

YOU'RE WELCOME FOR THE VIEW

WANNA
TOUCH
MY BUTT?

I'M A BUTT MODEL.
JEALOUS?

Made in the USA
Monee, IL
31 March 2021

64405418R00031